MEASURES *of* SUCCESS

A Comprehensive Musicianship Band Method

DEBORAH A. SHELDON • BRIAN BALMAGES • TIMOTHY LOEST • ROBERT SHELDON

PERCUSSION WRITTEN AND EDITED BY DAVID COLLIER

Welcome to *Measures of Success* and the amazing world of instrumental music! You are about to begin an exciting musical journey full of rewards and challenges. As you practice, you will find yourself sharing the gift of music with family, friends, and audiences. So get ready—your path to success begins now!

HISTORY OF THE BASSOON

The bassoon is the lowest sounding instrument in the woodwind family. It is referred to as a "double reed" instrument because its reed consists of two pieces of cane fastened together around a small metal tube. When played, the two reeds vibrate against each other to create the sound. The bassoon first appeared around 1650 with just finger holes and no keys. Later, keys were added to improve fingerings, which resulted in better tone quality and intonation. Today's bassoon uses the Heckel key mechanism developed in the 1800s. While early bassoons were made from a single piece of wood, today's bassoons are built in four sections using rosewood, maple or plastic. When assembled, the bassoon is about 4 feet tall. Unwound, its tubing is about 7.5 feet long. When first invented, the bassoon became a member of chamber ensembles and orchestras, generally covering the bass part. Later, it found a home in wind bands. While the bassoon can play quite low, the contrabassoon with its larger reed and double-length tubing sounds a complete octave lower.

Production: Frank J. Hackinson
Production Coordinators: Ken Mattis, Brian Balmages, and Philip Groeber
Cover Design and Interior Line Drawings: Danielle Taylor and Adrianne Hirosky
Interior Layout and Design: Andi Whitmer
Engraving: Tempo Music Press, Inc.
Printer: Tempo Music Press, Inc.

ISBN-13: 978-1-56939-805-0

THE FJH MUSIC COMPANY INC.
Frank J. Hackinson

BASSOON ASSEMBLY

BELL

BELL KEY

BOCAL

CORK

REED

BASS JOINT

WHISPER KEY PAD

WING JOINT

CORK

HAND REST

BOOT JOINT

Photograph courtesy of Yamaha Corporation of America

STEP 1
Lay your case flat on the floor. Open your case right side up.

STEP 2
Using the reed soaker cup, immerse entire reed in water.

STEP 3
With right hand, hold the boot joint away from key rods. With left hand, hold the wing joint away from key rods and insert it into the smaller boot joint opening.

STEP 4
Hold combined boot and wing joint with right hand at the boot joint. Hold bass joint with left hand and insert it into the larger boot joint opening.

STEP 5
Make sure that both wing and bass joints are fully inserted so that upper left hand thumb keys create a horseshoe pattern. Secure the body lock.

STEP 6
Holding the bass joint with the left hand, grasp the bell with the right hand and depress the top of the bell key to open the bridge key (low B♭ rod). Attach the bell.

STEP 7
Gently twist and insert bocal into top of wing joint, aligning the hole in bocal button with whisper key pad. Hold bocal at the curve so that it does not bend and kink.

STEP 8
Attach hand rest (crutch) and tighten screw. Use of the hand rest is optional, depending on the size of your hand.

STEP 9
Connect seat strap to boot joint.

STEP 10
Take reed from soaker cup, remove excess moisture, and place on bocal.

CHECK IT OUT!

POSTURE CHECKLIST
- Seat strap positioned toward front of chair
- Sit toward the back of the chair, but allow space for breathing
- Feet flat on the floor
- Sit straight and tall
- Shoulders relaxed
- Elbows comfortably away from your sides

HAND POSITION CHECKLIST
- Left thumb rests lightly on whisper key
- Palm of left hand steadies the bassoon at base of the index finger
- Left hand fingers 2 and 3 are slightly curved
- Right hand thumb rests lightly on the B♭ key
- Right hand fingers 1, 2 and 3 are poised to cover the front side keys and tone holes
- Right hand pinky gently rests on low F key

EMBOUCHURE CHECKLIST
- Reed is placed on the center of the lower lip
- Lips roll over the teeth
- Corners of the lips are forward (no smiling)
- Keep the space between your top and bottom teeth open (do not clench)
- Lips nearly touch the first wire of the reed

BASSOON SUPPLIES

• reeds   • reed case   • reed soaker cup   • swab   • bocal brush   • cork grease or canning wax   • soft cloth

BASSOON CARE

DAILY
- Blow excess moisture from reed and store in reed case
- Blow moisture out of bocal by blowing into large bocal opening
- Swab out inside of bassoon
- Wipe away moisture from tenon openings with soft cloth
- Wipe away fingerprints with soft cloth

EVERY TWO WEEKS—FOR BASSOONS WITH TENON CORKS
- Apply a thin coat of cork grease to tenon corks (wipe off old cork grease to prevent buildup)

MONTHLY—FOR BASSOONS WITH THREAD WRAPPED TENONS
- Soften a small cake of canning wax in your hands and rub a thin layer of wax onto the threads (never use cork grease)

YEARLY
- Take your bassoon to an authorized repair shop for a tune-up

NEVER
- Never submerge your bassoon in water
- Never apply cleaners or polishes to your bassoon
- Never adjust or oil your bassoon keys - leave this for a repair shop
- Never leave your bassoon unattended, or on the floor or chair
- Never expose your bassoon to extreme temperatures
- Never keep anything in your case except for your instrument, bocal, and supplies

BB208BSN

PRELUDE: SOUNDS BEFORE SYMBOLS

BREATHING

The key to playing a wind instrument well begins with taking a good breath. With just your reed,
take a full, relaxed breath and play a steady tone. How long can you hold it?

THEORY

PITCH, BEAT, AND RHYTHM

Pitch is the highness or lowness of a note or tone. The **beat** is the pulse of the music.
Rhythm is a pattern of short or long sounds (or silences) that fit with a steady beat.

ARTICULATION

Articulation is how the tongue and the air begin a note. Your director will show you how to articulate a note.

With just your reed, play some of the familiar songs below. Since you are only using your reed,
the *pitch* will stay the same, while the *rhythm* will identify the song. Articulate clearly!

Bingo	**Jingle Bells**	**London Bridge**
Mary Had a Little Lamb	**Old MacDonald**	**Twinkle, Twinkle Little Star**

MAKING MUSIC

With your director's help, assemble your entire bassoon carefully. You are now ready for your first three notes!

  NEW NOTE! D   **NEW NOTE! C**   **NEW NOTE! B♭**

Hold each note with a good sound until you are comfortable with it. Next, articulate each note four times and then rest for four beats.
Remember to focus on posture, hand position, and tone quality.

AND WE'RE OFF!

(hold) (rest)

D ———→ | – – – – | D D D D | – – – – | (repeat this with your other two new notes)
1 2 3 4   1 2 3 4   1 2 3 4   1 2 3 4

AU CLAIRE DE LA LUNE

B♭ B♭ B♭ C | D – C – | B♭ D C C | B♭ ——→ – – |
1 2 3 4   1 2 3 4   1 2 3 4   1 2 3 4

HOT CROSS BUNS

D ——→ C ——→ | B♭ ——→ – – | D ——→ C ——→ | B♭ ——→ – – | B♭ B♭ B♭ B♭ | C C C C | D ——→ C ——→ | B♭ ——→ – – |
1 2 3 4   1 2 3 4   1 2 3 4   1 2 3 4   1 2 3 4   1 2 3 4   1 2 3 4   1 2 3 4

MARY HAD A LITTLE LAMB

D C B♭ C | D D D – | C C C – | D D D – | D C B♭ C | D D D – | C C D C | B♭ ——→ – – |
1 2 3 4   1 2 3 4   1 2 3 4   1 2 3 4   1 2 3 4   1 2 3 4   1 2 3 4   1 2 3 4

COMPOSER'S CORNER

It is your turn to compose your *own* piece of music! Use the three notes you know to complete this piece.
Give it a title and perform it for a friend or family member!

Title:_____   Composer (your name):_____

B♭ __ __ __ | __ – __ – | __ __ __ – | __ __ B♭ – |

OPUS 1

THEORY

MUSIC STAFF

The **music staff** is where notes and rests are written. It has 5 lines and 4 spaces.

LONG TONE

A **long tone** is a held note. The fermata ($\frown$) indicates to hold the note until your teacher tells you to rest.

BAR LINES

Bar lines divide the music staff into measures.

FINAL BAR LINE

A **final bar** line indicates the end of a piece.

1.1 FIRST NOTE *Practice each long tone daily to improve your sound!*

TRACK 1 2

NEW NOTE! D

final bar line ↗

RHYTHM

BEAT

The **beat** is the pulse of the music. Tap your foot to keep a steady beat!

↓ ↑ ↓ ↑ ↓ ↑ ↓ ↑
1   **2**   **3**   **4**

NOTES AND RESTS

Notes represent sound. **Rests** represent silence.

♩   **Quarter Note** = 1 beat of sound

𝄽   **Quarter Rest** = 1 beat of silence

1.2 FOUR IN A ROW *This piece has four beats in each measure. Remember to tap your foot.*

TRACK 1 3

1   2   3   4   1   2   3   4   1   2   3   4   1   2   3   4   1   2   3   4

1.3 SECOND NOTE

TRACK 1 4

NEW NOTE! C

1.4 FOUR MORE *How many measures do you see?*

TRACK 1 5

1   2   3   4   1   2   3   4   1   2   3   4   1   2   3   4   1   2   3   4

1.5 UP AND DOWN *Any time you see a Bonus Box, write in the note name.*

TRACK 1 6

BONUS BOX

1.6 ALL MIXED UP

TRACK 1 7

BONUS BOX

BB208BSN

6

ACCIDENTALS

Accidentals are signs that alter a note's pitch. They are placed to the left of the note.

Flat (♭) A flat sign lowers the pitch by one half-step. This pitch remains lowered for the rest of the measure.

Sharp (♯) A sharp sign raises the pitch by one half-step. This pitch remains raised for the rest of the measure.

Natural (♮) A natural sign cancels a flat or sharp. It remains cancelled for the rest of the measure.

1.7 THIRD NOTE'S A CHARM

1.8 ALL TOGETHER

1.9 WHAT GOES UP...

1.10 RHYTHM RENDEZVOUS

CLEFS

Clefs are signs that help name notes.

The **bass clef**, also called the **F clef**, names F on the bass staff. The two dots appear on both sides of 4th line F. The musical alphabet uses A B C D E F and G. Each line and space of the staff has a note name. To find a bass clef note, move up or down by lines and spaces in the musical alphabet sequence.

LEDGER LINES

Ledger lines extend the staff. Notes written above or below the staff appear with ledger lines.

NAME THAT NOTE... *Use your knowledge of the musical alphabet to fill in the Bonus Boxes!*

HALF NOTES AND WHOLE NOTES

HALF RESTS AND WHOLE RESTS

TIME SIGNATURE

The top number shows the number of beats in each measure. The bottom number shows the type of note that receives one beat. *Hint: Replace the top number with a "1" and you will get a fraction that equals the type of note that gets one beat!*

Number of beats in a measure
Type of note that gets one beat

1.11 GOING PLACES *Circle the half rests.*

time signature

TRACK 1 12

1 2 3 4 1 2 3 4 1 2 3 4 1 2 3 4 1 2 3 4 1 2 3 4 1 2 3 4 1 2 3 4

FERMATA

When playing on your own, hold a note with a **fermata** longer than its assigned value.

1.12 COUNTDOWN *Hold the note with a fermata longer than its assigned value.*

fermata

TRACK 1 13

1 2 3 4   1 2 3 4

REPEAT SIGN

A **repeat sign** is a final bar line with two dots. Without stopping, go back to the beginning and play the music a second time.

1.13 TURN AROUND *Say the note names and demonstrate your fingerings before you play.*

TRACK 1 14

repeat sign

1.14 HOT CROSS BUNS

English Folk Song

TRACK 1 15

1.15 HERE WE GO! *Draw in the bar lines, then play!*

BONUS BOX

TRACK 1 16

BB208BSN

THEORY

PHRASING

A **phrase** in music is similar to a sentence in speech. It should continue uninterrupted until the music indicates a breath.

, A **breath mark** indicates to take a breath through your mouth.

1.24 DOWN BY THE STATION

American Folk Song

breath mark → **,**

HISTORY

MUSIC

Stephen Collins Foster (1826 – 1864) was an American songwriter born in Pennsylvania. He published his first piece when he was 18 years old. Some of his most famous songs are *Oh! Susanna, Camptown Races,* and *Some Folks Do.* His compositions capture the spirit of American folk music during the 1800s.

ART

During this time in history, artists of the Hudson River School were hard at work in the United States. Frederic Church painted *Morning, Looking East Over the Hudson Valley from the Catskill Mountains* about the same time that *Camptown Races* was written.

WORLD

The world was introduced to Ebenezer Scrooge (the famous character in Charles Dickens' *A Christmas Carol*), Abraham Lincoln delivered the Gettysburg Address, and the stapler was patented.

1.25 SOME FOLKS DO ✏️ *Before you play, draw these symbols where they belong: Bass Clef, Time Signature, Final Bar Line.*

Stephen C. Foster

1.26 SCALING THE WALL *Work with another student to learn this piece.*

BONUS BOX

CONDUCTING IN $\frac{4}{4}$ TIME

ON THE PODIUM

Your band director has been conducting a four-beat pattern. Now it is your turn to conduct! Place your right hand in a "handshake" position and follow the diagram to conduct in $\frac{4}{4}$ time.

1.27 GOOD KING WENCESLAS *Conduct a partner, your section, or the entire class!*

English Carol

ON THE PODIUM

1.28 STOMP ROCK

stomp

BB208BSN

OPUS 1 ENCORE!

INTERPRETATION STATION

TRACK 1 30

Listen to CD 1 Track 30. Describe the music and how it makes you feel.

SIMON "SEZ"

Your director will give you a starting note. Listen to the rhythms your director plays and echo them back. Listen carefully!

COMPOSER'S CORNER

A composer is someone who creates original music. It is YOUR turn to be a composer!
Using the notes you already know, complete this composition. Guide rhythms have been provided for you in parentheses.

Title:_____ Name:_____

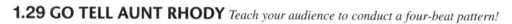

PENCIL POWER

Match the following terms with their symbols.

1. _____ Clef
2. _____ Time Signature
3. _____ Repeat Sign
4. _____ Fermata
5. _____ Half Note

6. _____ Quarter Note
7. _____ Whole Note
8. _____ Whole Rest
9. _____ Half Rest
10. _____ Quarter Rest

A: :| B: 𝄽   C: 4/4   D: ▬

E: 𝅝   F: ▬   G: 𝄐   H: 𝅗𝅥

I: 𝄢   J: 𝅘𝅥

CURTAIN UP!

Time to perform! Practice these pieces and play them for friends or family members. Introduce each piece by its title.
Remember to bow when you are finished!

1.29 GO TELL AUNT RHODY *Teach your audience to conduct a four-beat pattern!*

American Folk Song

TRACK 1 31

1.30 CUCKOO SAMBA

TRACK 1 32

1.31 LIGHTLY ROW — Duet *Pair up with a friend to perform this piece for your audience. Switch parts on the repeat!*

Traditional

TRACK 1 33

BB208BSN

✸ OPUS 2

HISTORY

MUSIC

Ludwig van Beethoven (1770 – 1827) lived most of his life in Vienna, Austria. His music became a bridge between Classical and Romantic music. When *Symphony No. 9* and its *Ode to Joy* were performed for the first time, Beethoven was completely deaf!

ART

Romanticism in art was an important movement in Europe and themes often included nationalism. Eugene Delacroix was one of the most important French artists. His *Liberty Leading the People* commemorates the French Revolution of 1830 and the overthrow of King Charles X.

WORLD

Around this time in history, Mexico became a republic, trains first carried passengers in England, the first photograph was taken, and ice cream was first sold in the United States!

2.1 ODE TO JOY *Musicianship Challenge! – Without the CD, play the 1ˢᵗ phrase gently, the 2ⁿᵈ phrase majestically.*

Ludwig van Beethoven   TRACK 1 · 34

2.2 OUTER LIMITS   TRACK 1 · 35

NEW NOTE! G

2.3 OLD MACDONALD

American Folk Song   TRACK 1 · 36

continue to the next line

2.4 SHARK! *Musicianship Challenge! – Without the CD, play this like you are being chased.*

TRACK 1 · 37

NEW NOTE! A

Choose any note you have learned!

2.5 CRUSADER'S HYMN *Play each phrase in one breath.*

Silesian Folk Song   TRACK 1 · 38

THEORY

KEY SIGNATURE

The **key signature** indicates which notes to play sharp or flat. It appears at the beginning of each staff.

- There can be up to 7 sharps in a key signature.   **Sharps** (♯) follow this order: F, C, G, D, A, E, B
- There can be up to 7 flats in a key signature.   **Flats** (♭) follow this order: B, E, A, D, G, C, F
- Your key signature in 2.6, *Keynote March,* indicates that all Bs and Es should be played as B-flats and E-flats.

This is the key of B♭ Major.

2.6 KEYNOTE MARCH *Musicianship Challenge! – Play this piece like you would hear it in a parade.*

TRACK 1 · 39

key signature

HISTORY

MUSIC
Wolfgang Amadeus Mozart (1756 – 1791) was born in Salzburg, Austria. He was a child genius and composed his first minuet when he was just five years old! During his short life of 35 years, he wrote over 600 musical compositions. Many of his works continue to be performed today.

ART
As Mozart wrote in the Classical style, Neoclassicism in visual art was being explored by artists such as Jacques-Louis David, a French painter. This style can be seen in his painting, *The Death of Socrates,* which was completed in 1787.

WORLD
The thirteen American Colonies broke away from the British Empire in the American Revolutionary War, the *Declaration of Independence* was signed, and Johnny Appleseed was born.

2.7 STAR SEARCH *This piece is in the key of _____ Major.*

French Melody
adapted by Wolfgang A. Mozart — TRACK 1/40

THEORY

DYNAMICS
Dynamics indicate how loudly or softly to play. Italian terms are often used in music to indicate volume.

p (*piano*) – play softly f (*forte*) – play loudly

2.8 BEAT STREET *Clap the rhythm with dynamics!*

CLAP — TRACK 1/41

2.9 LONDON BRIDGE *Show phrasing by placing breath marks in this piece before you play it.*

English Folk Song — TRACK 1/42

2.10 JINGLE BELLS – Duet

James Pierpont — TRACK 1/43

BB208BSN

ON THE PODIUM

When dynamics indicate *loud*, a conductor's gestures are bigger.
When dynamics indicate *soft*, gestures are smaller.
Practice conducting a four-beat pattern with dynamics!

2.11 DREIDEL SONG

Traditional Hannukah Song — TRACK 1 · 44

THEORY
DYNAMICS

Mezzo is an Italian term that means "medium" or "moderately." The letter *m* is an abbreviation used in dynamics.
mp (*mezzo piano*) – play moderately soft   *mf* (*mezzo forte*) – play moderately loud

2.12 BEAT STREET *Clap the dynamics!*

TRACK 1 · 45

CLAP

2.13 DYNAMIC DOODLE ALL DAY

American Folk Melody — TRACK 1 · 46

THEORY
PICK-UP NOTES

Pick-up notes lead into the first full measure of a phrase.
When pick-up notes are used to begin a piece, their combined rhythmic value is often subtracted from the last measure.

2.14 A–TISKET, A–TASKET

American Folk Song — TRACK 1 · 47

2.15 OH! SUSANNA – Duet

Stephen C. Foster — TRACK 1 · 48

14

2.16 AFRICAN SAFARI

ARTICULATION: ACCENT

An **accent** indicates to emphasize a note by playing louder. Use your air!

2.17 LEAN ON IT

2.18 WALK TO MY LOU

American Folk Melody

SYNCOPATION

Music has strong beats and weak beats. Most of the time, we stress strong beats (**1** 2 **3** 4).
Sometimes, we shift the stress onto weak beats (1 **2** 3 **4**).
This is known as **syncopation**. Longer, accented notes that occur on weak beats often identify syncopation.

2.19 BEAT STREET

2.20 SHOO FLY

American Folk Song

2.21 CHANT

OPUS 2 ENCORE!

INTERPRETATION STATION

Listen to CD 1 Track 55. You will hear two performances of the same piece. Which one is more musical and why?

SIMON "SEZ"

Listen to CD 1 Track 56. You will hear a well-known song. Listen first, sing it, then find the pitches on your instrument. You can then play along with the accompaniment track that follows. Can you match the initial recording?

COMPOSER'S CORNER

Use the notes and rhythms you have learned to complete the composition. Be sure to give it a title!

Title:_____ Name:_____

PENCIL POWER

The Secret Decoder: Name the notes and solve the puzzles!

Beethoven went ___ ___ ___ ___ towards the end of his life.

The ___ ___ ___ ___ in the ___ ___ ___ ___ photo h___ ___ ___ ___ ___ ___ ___ with time.

H___ h___ ___ to pay an extra ___ ___ ___ for the ___ i ___ ___ ___ ___ ___ ___ ___ .

He ___ ___ ___ ___ ___ when he mistakenly ate ___ ___ ___ corned ___ ___ ___ ___ and ___ ___ ___ ___ ___ ___ ___ ___ !

CURTAIN UP!

2.22 TOKECANG

Traditional Indonesian

CURTAIN UP! FIRST CONCERT

2.23 CONCERT WARM–UP NO. 1 TRACK 1 58

2.24 CONCERT WARM–UP NO. 2 TRACK 1 59

2.25 THE SYNCOPATED ROW BOAT – Duet Traditional Melody TRACK 1 60

2.26 CROWN OF MAJESTY – Full Band Robert Sheldon TRACK 1 61

9 ← *rehearsal number*

2.27 OBWISANA – Duet or Full Band with Percussion Ghanian Folk Song TRACK 1 62

2.28 FANFARE FOR A WINTER CELEBRATION – Full Band

arr. Brian Balmages

TRACK 1 63

2.29 THE SECTION BATTLE RAG – Full Band

Brian Balmages

TRACK 1 64

16 Section Feature!
Circle the measure(s) your director asks you to play! - - - - - - - - - - - - - - tutti (everyone)

2.30 ON CARIBBEAN SHORES (MARY ANN) – Full Band

Jamaican Folk Song
arr. Robert Sheldon

TRACK 1 65

2.31 ROCK THE HOUSE – Full Band

Brian Balmages

TRACK 1 66

✳ OPUS 3

MORE TIME SIGNATURES

RHYTHM
13

$\frac{3}{4}$ **3 beats** in each measure
Quarter note gets one beat

$\frac{2}{4}$ **2 beats** in each measure
Quarter note gets one beat

3.1 BEAT STREET
TRACK 1 67

3.2 THREE'S A CROWD
TRACK 1 68

3.3 THREE POINTER
TRACK 1 69

3.4 BEAT STREET
TRACK 1 70

3.5 RAIN, RAIN, GO AWAY
Traditional TRACK 1 71

ON THE PODIUM

CONDUCTING IN $\frac{2}{4}$ TIME

It is your turn to conduct a two-beat pattern.
With your right hand in a "handshake" position,
follow the diagram to conduct in $\frac{2}{4}$ time.

3.6 TWO FOR YOU
TRACK 1 72

3.7 TERRIBLE TWOS
TRACK 1 73

BB208BSN

REVISITING ACCIDENTALS

THEORY

Accidentals include **flat** (♭), **sharp** (♯), and **natural** (♮) signs found in front of notes, but not in the key signature.
A flat sign (♭) lowers the pitch one half-step. It remains in effect for the rest of the measure.

3.8 CANYONS

NEW KEY SIGNATURE

THEORY

This is the key of E♭ Major.

This key signature indicates that all Bs, Es, and As should be played as B-flats, E-flats, and A-flats.

3.9 ROYAL SCEPTER *Musicianship Challenge! – Play this piece in a noble style.*

3.10 THINGS ARE LOOKING UP *Add a breath mark after the first phrase.*

THE RULE OF THE DOT

RHYTHM

Adding a dot after a note increases the length of the note **by half its value.**
When adding a dot to a half note, it becomes a **dotted half note.**

2 beats + 1 beat = 3 beats   2 beats + 1 beat = 3 beats   1 2 3

3.11 BEAT STREET

CLAP

Begin CD 2

3.12 TRIPLE CROWN

3.13 MINUET

Daniel G. Türk

BB208BSN

20

3.14 JUNGLE RITUAL

f   *mp*   *f*

3.15 VOLGA BOATMEN *p–f* Play *piano* the first time and *forte* the second time.

Russian Folk Song

p–f

3.16 SHE WORE A YELLOW RIBBON

Traditional American

mf

3.17 CAMPTOWN RACES – Duet

Stephen C. Foster

A   *f*

B   *f*

EIGHTH NOTES

Eighth Note = half beat of sound

Flagged Eighth Notes   1 + 2 +

Beamed Eighth Notes   1 + 2 +

3.18 BEAT STREET *Tap your foot to keep a steady beat!*

1 + 2 + 3 + 4 +   1 + 2 + 3 + 4 +   1 + 2 + 3 + 4 +   1 + 2 + 3 + 4 +

3.19 EIGHTH NOTE EXPRESS

1 + 2 + 3 + 4 +   1 + 2 + 3 + 4 +   1 + 2 + 3 + 4 +   1 + 2 + 3 + 4 +

COMMON TIME

𝄴   The **common time** symbol means the same thing as 4/4 time.

3.20 GRANDMA GRUNTS

Traditional American

common time

mf

BB208BSN

3.21 SKIP TO MY LOU

American Folk Song

TRACK 2 11

WHOLE MEASURE REST

Rest for the entire measure. Check the time signature!

3.22 WALTZING LOU *How should you play these dynamics?*

American Folk Melody

TRACK 2 12

(1 - 2 - 3)

ENCLOSED REPEAT SIGNS

Repeat the music between the two signs.

3.23 TWO BY FOUR

TRACK 2 13

STYLE AND FORM: ROUND

In a **round**, each musician plays the same part, but enters at a different time.

3.24 FRÉRE JACQUES – Round *As each musician reaches ②, the next musician should begin playing at ①.*

French Folk Song

TRACK 2 14

STYLE AND FORM: THEME AND VARIATIONS

Composers create a **variation** when they change a melody in some way. Changes can be made to the notes, rhythm, key, and even the time signature! While you will notice the differences in each variation, you will still be able to recognize the original theme.

A **double bar line** indicates the end of one section and the beginning of another.

3.25 VARIATIONS ON A FRENCH MELODY

TRACK 2 15

Theme

Variation 1

Variation 2

22

DYNAMICS

Crescendo means to gradually play louder.   **Decrescendo** means to gradually play softer.

3.26 IT'S SWELL *Clap first, then play!*
TRACK 2 16

3.27 OUTTA MY WAY
TRACK 2 17

3.28 REGAL FANFARE
TRACK 2 18

NEW NOTE! F

HISTORY

MUSIC

German born **George Frideric Handel** (1685 – 1759) composed many types of music including oratorios, operas, and orchestral works. *Music for the Royal Fireworks* was written when George II of Great Britain hired him to write music to accompany fireworks in London. The event commemorated the signing of the Treaty of Aix-la-Chapelle in 1749.

ART

During colonial times, American painting and drawing focused on portraiture. Joseph Badger painted portraits of prominent figures and children in colonial Boston. His style can be seen in the portrait of *Jeremiah Belknap*, painted in 1758.

WORLD

Sir Isaac Newton stated the three universal laws of motion. In the same publication he used the Latin word *gravitas* that would become known as gravity. Also, America founded its first hospital in Pennsylvania.

3.29 MUSIC FOR THE ROYAL FIREWORKS
George F. Handel   TRACK 2 19

BEAM GROUPS

3.30 SCALE THE WALL
TRACK 2 20

3.31 NEW FRONTIERS

3.32 THE SAINTS GO MARCHING IN *Pick-up notes lead into measure 1.*

Traditional Spiritual

CONDUCTING IN ¾ TIME

It is your turn to conduct a three-beat pattern. With your right hand in a "handshake" position, follow the diagram to conduct in ¾ time.

3.33 ROLLING ALONG

FIRST AND SECOND ENDINGS

At the **first ending**, play through it to the repeat sign. Go back to the beginning or the previous repeat sign and play again. Skip the first ending – play the **second ending** instead.

second time

3.34 LONG, LONG AGO

Traditional

3.35 JOLLY OLD SAINT NICHOLAS – Duet

American Carol

A

B

OPUS 3 ENCORE!

INTERPRETATION STATION

Listen to CD 2 Track 26. You will hear four musical examples, all composed using a different time signature.
As you listen, pay close attention to how rhythmic ideas are grouped. Circle the correct time signature for each example.

1. $\frac{3}{4}$ $\frac{4}{4}$ 2. $\frac{2}{4}$ $\frac{3}{4}$ 3. $\frac{3}{4}$ $\frac{4}{4}$ 4. $\frac{2}{4}$ $\frac{3}{4}$

SIMON "SEZ"

TRACK 2 27

Listen to CD 2 Track 27. You are going to hear a piece called *One Note Wonder*. It gets its title because it uses only one pitch!
You will hear dynamics that make it very interesting. Play along with the accompaniment track that follows, imitating the dynamics
and rhythm of the initial recording to make it musical.

COMPOSER'S CORNER

It is your turn to be a composer again! Use notes and rhythms you have learned to complete each measure (remember to
look at the time signature). Then give your piece a title and perform it for a friend or family member!

Title:_____ Name:_____

PENCIL POWER

Each measure below is rhythmically incomplete! For each example, add *one note* to complete the measure and make it correct.

    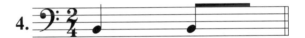

CURTAIN UP!

3.36 ZUM GALI GALI – Round

Traditional Hebrew Song TRACK 2 28

3.37 DRY BONES

Spiritual TRACK 2 29

CURTAIN UP!

OPUS 4

4.1 CIRCUS ACT

NEW NOTE!
E

4.2 DAYBREAK

ON THE PODIUM

Legato *(smooth and flowing)*

THEORY

NEW KEY SIGNATURE

This is the key of **F Major**

This key signature indicates that all Bs should be played as B-flats.

4.3 CHIAPANECAS

Mexican Folk Song

BONUS BOX

new key signature

stomp

THEORY

ARTICULATION: SLUR

A **slur** is a curved line that connects notes of *different* pitches. Tongue only the first note of a slur.

4.4 SLURRED NOT SHAKEN

NEW NOTE!
A

Legato

4.5 SLIP 'N' SLIDE

TEMPO

THEORY

Tempo is the speed of the beat. Music can move at different rates of speed.

Largo – a slow tempo   **Moderato** – a medium tempo   **Allegro** – a fast tempo

4.6 MUSETTE

J.S. Bach — TRACK 2 37

Moderato

4.7 CIELITO LINDO

Mexican Folk Song — TRACK 2 38

Allegro

ON THE PODIUM

HISTORY

MUSIC

Gustav Mahler (1860 – 1911) was a noted composer and conductor of the late Romantic era. He spent time in New York conducting the Metropolitan Opera and the New York Philharmonic Orchestra. He is mainly known for his large symphonies (his *Symphony No. 8* uses over a thousand performers!).

ART

The world saw the emergence of Cubism, a style in which objects were broken up, then reassembled in abstract forms. Pablo Picasso became one of the most famous Cubists in history. His *Ma Jolie* (1911) is an early example of the style.

WORLD

Mark Twain published *The Adventures of Tom Sawyer*, Sir Arthur Conan Doyle introduced the world to Sherlock Holmes, and the coin-operated telephone was invented.

4.8 THEME FROM SYMPHONY NO. 1 – Round

Gustav Mahler — TRACK 2 39

Largo

RHYTHM

TIE

A **tie** is a curved line that connects notes of the *same* pitch. These notes are "tied" together and played to sound like one longer note.

4.9 MAKING CONNECTIONS

TRACK 2 40

4.10 ALL TIED UP

TRACK 2 41

BB208BSN

HISTORY

MUSIC

Pyotr Ilyich Tchaikovsky (1840 – 1893) was a Russian composer who studied music at a very young age. His most famous works include the ballet *The Nutcracker* and the exciting *1812 Overture*. He composed *Capriccio Italien* after a visit to Italy during Carnivale season.

ART

In 1880, the Arts and Crafts Movement was going strong in England. This style is reflected in art, architecture, and interior design. Works by British architect Herbert Tudor Buckland and American architect Frank Lloyd Wright are typical of the Arts and Crafts style.

WORLD

Wabash, Indiana became the first town to be completely illuminated using electric light and the Statue of Liberty was presented to the United States by the people of France.

4.11 CAPRICCIO ITALIEN *How many slurs are in this piece?*

Pyotr I. Tchaikovsky

TRACK 2 42

4.12 BARCAROLLE

Jacques Offenbach

TRACK 2 43

NEW NOTE!
Db

THEORY

NEW KEY SIGNATURE

This is the key of A♭ **Major.**

This key signature indicates that all Bs, Es, As, and Ds should be played as B-flats, E-flats, A-flats, and D-flats.

4.13 THE BLUE BELLS OF SCOTLAND

Scottish Folk Song

TRACK 2 44

HISTORY

MUSIC

John Philip Sousa (1854 – 1932) was a violinist, composer, and conductor born in Washington, D.C. He conducted the United States Marine Band from 1880 until 1892. His marches, such as *The Stars and Stripes Forever, Semper Fidelis*, and the *Liberty Bell*, are well known and important to American culture.

ART

In the early 20th century, artist Salvador Dali of Spain was mostly known as a surrealist and emphasized visions of the subconscious. *The Persistence of Memory* (1931), a scene with melting clocks, is one of his best known works.

WORLD

Elsewhere in 1917, the Russian revolution began, World War I was still raging, and the first commercial recordings of jazz music were available to the public.

4.14 HIGH SCHOOL CADETS

John Philip Sousa

TRACK 2 45

4.15 IT'S ONLY NATURAL

TRACK 2 46

4.16 ACCIDENTAL BLUES – Duet

TRACK 2 47

courtesy accidental

RETURN OF THE DOT RULE

Adding a dot after a note increases the length of the note by half its value. Here, the dot is used with a quarter note to create a **dotted quarter note**.

4.17 BEAT STREET *Tap your foot to keep a steady beat.*

TRACK 2 48

1 + 2 + 3 + 4 +   1 + 2 + 3 + 4 +   1 + 2 + 3 + 4 +   1 + 2 + 3 + 4 +

4.18 DOTS A LOT

TRACK 2 49

1 + 2 + 3 + 4 +   1 + 2 + 3 + 4 +   1 + 2 + 3 + 4 +   1 + 2 + 3 + 4 +

RITARDANDO

Ritardando – abbreviated "*rit.*" – means to make the tempo gradually slower.

4.19 ALL THROUGH THE NIGHT

Welsh Folk Song

TRACK 2 50

Dolce

1.   2. *rit.*

p - mp

30

4.20 AMERICA

Maestoso

Traditional

TRACK 2 51

D.C. AL FINE

D.C. is an abbreviation for *da capo*, an Italian term that refers to the beginning.
At the **D.C. al Fine**, return to the beginning and play again until the **Fine**.

4.21 ALOUETTE

Moderato

French-Canadian Folk Song

TRACK 2 52

4.22 BANANA BOAT SONG *Calypso is a blend of African and Caribbean music.*

Calypso

Caribbean Folk Song

TRACK 2 53

MUSIC

Antonín Dvořák (1841 – 1904) was from a small town near Prague, in the Czech Republic. He eventually moved to the United States and became the director of the New York Conservatory of Music. In 1888, the Conservatory welcomed African-Americans while other schools were still practicing segregation. His *Symphony No. 9* (*"From the New World"*) was composed during his brief time in America. It is influenced by Native American music and African-American spirituals.

ART

French artist Georges Seurat painted *A Sunday Afternoon on the Island of La Grande Jatte*. This large painting, depicting a scene of recreation in Paris, was created using a technique called pointillism. Composed entirely of painted dots, it took him nearly two years to finish.

WORLD

Congress abolished slavery in the U.S. Territories, Albert Einstein was born, the World's Columbian Exposition was held in Chicago, and New York became the first state to require license plates on cars.

4.23 THEME FROM THE NEW WORLD SYMPHONY

Largo

Antonín Dvořák

TRACK 2 54

RHYTHM 13

MORE ABOUT THE DOT

While a dotted quarter note is usually followed by an eighth note, the eighth note sometimes appears *before* the dotted quarter note.

4.24 BEAT STREET
TRACK 2 55

4.25 CARIBBEAN CARNIVAL
TRACK 2 56
Calypso

4.26 GOOD NIGHT LADIES
Traditional TRACK 2 57
Brightly

4.27 GOING TO KENTUCKY
American Folk Song TRACK 2 58
Allegro

4.28 FILL 'ER UP *A deep breath and full airstream will help you play with a beautiful sound.*
TRACK 2 59

4.29 MARCHE MILITAIRE
Franz Schubert TRACK 2 60
Marziale *(in a march style)*

BB208BSN

OPUS 4 ENCORE!

INTERPRETATION STATION

TRACK 2 61

Listen to CD 2 Track 61. For each example, decide if the tempo is *Largo*, *Moderato*, or *Allegro*.
Circle the correct answer.

1. L M A   2. L M A   3. L M A   4. L M A

SIMON "SEZ"

TRACK 2 62

Listen to CD 2 Track 62. You are going to hear the same five-note pattern articulated four different ways.
Match the performance to its correctly notated example. The first one has been done for you!

No. 1 = __B__   No. 2 = ____   No. 3 = ____   No. 4 = ____

COMPOSER'S CORNER

Sometimes a composer takes an existing melody and presents it in a new way. This is called **arranging**. Change the rhythms of the music in *Alouette in Four* so it is playable in $\frac{2}{4}$ time. *Hint: Cut the rhythmic value of each note in half!* The arrangement has been started for you.

ALOUETTE IN FOUR

ALOUETTE IN TWO

PENCIL POWER – MATCH THE COMPOSER

Match the composer with the correct fact by writing in the appropriate letter.

_____ Wolfgang Amadeus Mozart

_____ Antonín Dvořák

_____ Gustav Mahler

_____ John Philip Sousa

_____ Ludwig van Beethoven

_____ Pyotr Ilyich Tchaikovsky

A.   Russian composer who wrote the famous ballet, *The Nutcracker*

B.   U.S. Marine Band conductor and composer known for his marches

C.   His *Symphony No. 9* reveals the influence of African-American spirituals

D.   Child genius who composed over 600 works in a short life of 35 years

E.   Continued to compose music after becoming completely deaf

F.   Composer of the late Romantic era known for his large symphonies

CURTAIN UP!

4.30 HAVA NASHIRA – Round

Israeli Folk Song   **TRACK 2 63**

CURTAIN UP! FULL BAND

4.31 LITTLE SWALLOW

Chinese Folk Song
arr. Robert Sheldon

TRACK 2 64

4.32 FURY *divisi (div.) – Part of the section plays the top note and part of the section plays the bottom note.*

Brian Balmages

TRACK 2 65

BB208BSN

4.33 HAIL THE CONQUERING HERO
Instrumental Solo

George F. Handel
arr. Brian Balmages

Piano Accompaniment

OPUS 5

In this Opus, focus on breath support and sound. Strive to hold all notes for their full value, especially those connected by a slur or tie.

Begin CD 3

5.1 CATAPULT! TRACK 3 1

5.2 UP AND OVER TRACK 3 2

5.3 SMOOTH HORIZONS TRACK 3 3

5.4 UP, UP AND AWAY! TRACK 3 4

5.5 CLIMB ON TRACK 3 5

5.6 OVER EASY TRACK 3 6

5.7 ZERO GRAVITY TRACK 3 7

5.8 BREAKING THROUGH TRACK 3 8

5.9 THE MOON TURNS DARK French Folk Melody TRACK 3 9

Misterioso *(mysteriously)*

BB208BSN

36

BB208BSN

MUSIC

German composer **Johannes Brahms** (1833 – 1897) was also an accomplished pianist and gave the first performance of many of his own works. *Lullaby (Wiegenlied)* was composed in 1868 to celebrate the birth of his friend's son.

ART

In the mid 1800s, Realists were concerned with objectivity. American artist James Whistler titled many of his works "harmonies" or "arrangements." An example is his *Arrangement in Grey and Black No. 1: Portrait of the Artist's Mother.*

WORLD

In 1868, floats appeared in New Orleans' Mardi Gras parade for the first time and the first Memorial Day was celebrated in the United States.

5.17 LULLABY – Duet

Cantabile *(in a singing style)*

Johannes Brahms

EIGHTH RESTS

The **eighth rest** receives one-half beat in $\frac{4}{4}$ time.

Eighth rests can replace upbeat eighth notes.   Eighth rests can replace downbeat eighth notes.

5.18 BEAT STREET

5.19 SCALING WITH EIGHTH RESTS

MUSIC

German composer **Johann Sebastian Bach** (1685 – 1750) began learning music as a young boy, studying violin and organ. He is thought to be one of the greatest composers who ever lived. His work is the model of the Baroque style.

ART

Peter Paul Rubens painted a series of works in the Baroque Style for Marie de Medici at the Luxembourg Palace in Paris, France. These works are now on display at the Louvre, one of the most famous art museums in the world.

WORLD

The tuning fork was invented by Englishman John Shore, the first folding umbrella was manufactured in France, and infamous pirate Edward Teach (Blackbeard) terrorized people along the Atlantic coast.

5.20 MINUET NO. 1

Moderato

J. S. Bach

38

5.21 BEAT STREET

5.22 STEPPIN' OFF THE EIGHTH

5.23 TIPTOE TANGO *Tango is a type of music and dance that originated in Buenos Aires, Argentina.*

5.24 ROCK ON, ROCK OFF – Duet

THEORY
ARTICULATION: TENUTO AND STACCATO

Tenuto
Play with full value.

Staccato
Play light and separated.

5.25 LONG AND SHORT OF IT
TRACK 3 25

HISTORY

MUSIC
Austrian composer **Franz Joseph Haydn** (1732 – 1809) is often referred to as the father of the symphony (He wrote 108 of them!). *Symphony No. 94* is often called the *Surprise Symphony*. Haydn surprised listeners with an unexpected loud chord that came after some very quiet music.

ART
Americans saw paintings by countryman John Trumbull (his historical painting *Declaration of Independence* is on the back of the $2 bill). In England, young artist Joseph Turner was setting the tone for Impressionism.

WORLD
The United States Bill of Rights was ratified, the world's first Sunday newspaper (*The Observer*) was published in England, and Benjamin Franklin invented bifocals!

5.26 SURPRISE SYMPHONY
Franz J. Haydn — TRACK 3 26

Andante

HISTORY

MUSIC
Paul Abraham Dukas (1865 – 1935) was a French composer who wrote in the Romantic style. His most famous work, *The Sorcerer's Apprentice,* is based on a poem by Johann Wolfgang von Goethe. The poem describes an apprentice who loses control of an enchanted broomstick.

ART
Edvard Munch, from Norway, painted in the Expressionist style which uses symbolism to portray many different themes. One of his best-known works is *The Scream* (1893).

WORLD
The 19th Amendment gave women the right to vote, author Madeleine L'Engle was born, and the first underground metro railway opened in Boston.

5.27 THE SORCERER'S APPRENTICE
Paul A. Dukas — TRACK 3 27

Misterioso

5.28 GO DOWN MOSES
Spiritual — TRACK 3 28

NEW NOTE! Gb

5.29 JITTERS, CRITTERS
TRACK 3 29

Misterioso

BB208BSN

OPUS 5 ENCORE! ✳

INTERPRETATION STATION

TRACK 3 / 30

Listen to CD 3 Track 30. For each example, decide if the articulation is *Legato* or *Staccato*.
Circle the letter that corresponds with your answer.

1. L S   2. L S   3. L S   4. L S

SIMON "SEZ"

TRACK 3 / 31

Listen to CD 3 Track 31. You will hear a well-known song. Listen first, sing it, then find the pitches on your instrument. You can then play along with the accompaniment track that follows. Can you match the notes and style of the initial recording?

COMPOSER'S CORNER

Writing a theme is just one part of a composer's process. Composers also use dynamics to make their music more expressive.
Add your own dynamics and then play the piece expressively. Choose from the following:

p mp mf f 〈 〉

PENCIL POWER – MATCH THE STYLE TERMS

Match the style term with the correct definition by writing in the appropriate letter.

_____ Legato	A. In a singing style
_____ Maestoso	B. In a march style
_____ Dolce	C. Smooth and flowing
_____ Marziale	D. Sweetly
_____ Cantabile	E. Blend of African and Caribbean music
_____ Calypso	F. Majestically

CURTAIN UP!

5.30 LOCH LOMOND

Scottish Folk Song   **TRACK 3 / 32**

Cantabile

CURTAIN UP! FULL BAND

5.31 LA MORISQUE (RENAISSANCE DANCE)

Tielman Susato
arr. Brian Balmages
TRACK 3 33

5.32 COSSACK'S MARCHING SONG

Russian Folk Song
arr. Robert Sheldon
TRACK 3 34

BB208BSN

✳ OPUS 6

ENHARMONICS

Two notes that have the same pitch but different names are called **enharmonics**. An example would be G♭ and F♯.
They have different names but share the same fingering and sound the same when played!

6.1 ENHARMONIC ZONE

6.2 THE SPHINX

6.3 THE SPY

6.4 FINAL FRONTIER

6.5 MARCH SLAV

Maestoso

Pyotr I. Tchaikovsky

DYNAMICS

pp (*pianissimo*) – play very soft

ff (*fortissimo*) – play very loud

6.6 ARIRANG

Andante

Korean Folk Song

HISTORY

MUSIC
Italian born **Giuseppe Verdi** (1813 – 1901) is best known for his operas, especially *Il Trovatore* (The Troubadour), first performed in 1853. The *Anvil Chorus*, from Act 2 of *Il Trovatore*, features Spanish gypsies who sing and strike anvils as they work in the early morning.

ART
Art in the style of Luminism began in the 1850s and was characterized by the use of light effects best seen in sea and landscapes. This American style is found in works by Frederic Church (*Twilight in the Wilderness*) and Martin Heade (*Sunlight and Shadow: The Newbury Marshes*).

WORLD
In 1853, when *Il Trovatore* premiered, the Ottoman Empire declared war on Russia, the Gadsden Purchase (currently southern Arizona and New Mexico) was made, and potato chips made their first tasty appearance.

6.7 ANVIL CHORUS
Pesante *(heavily)*

Giuseppe Verdi TRACK 3 41

THEORY

MORE DYNAMICS

cresc. Sometimes this abbreviation is used in place of a crescendo sign. It means the same thing as the sign; gradually play louder.

decresc. Sometimes this abbreviation is used in place of a decrescendo sign. It means the same thing as the sign; gradually play softer.

6.8 YANKEE DOODLE CAME AND WENT
Moderato

American Folk Melody TRACK 3 42

THEORY

MAJOR SCALE, ARPEGGIO, AND CHORD

A **major scale** has eight notes going up or down in consecutive order, all in the key signature of the scale name. In your key of B♭ Major, all eight notes are in the key signature of B♭ Major, which has 2 flats. The top and bottom notes are both B♭. The distance between these notes is called an **octave**.

An **arpeggio** is the first, third, and fifth notes of a scale played in *succession*. It may also include the 8th scale note.

A **major chord** is the first, third, and fifth notes of a major scale played *simultaneously*. Like the arpeggio, it may also include the 8th scale note.

6.9 CONCERT B♭ MAJOR SCALE

TRACK 3 43

6.10 CONCERT B♭ MAJOR ARPEGGIO AND CHORD

TRACK 3 44

44

6.11 KUM BAH YAH *Circle the arpeggios.*

mp   *pp*   *mp* cresc.   *mf* decresc.   *pp*

THEORY
INTERVALS

An **interval** is the distance between two pitches. You can figure out the interval by counting each line and space between the notes. Starting with "1" on the bottom note, count upward until you reach the top note. The number of the top note identifies the interval.

unison   2nd   3rd   4th   5th   6th   7th   octave

6.12 RANGE ROVER *Identify each interval, counting from the bottom note.*

TRACK 3 46

ON THE PODIUM

6.13 HATIKVAH

Israeli National Anthem   TRACK 3 47

Andante

mp   1.   2.

6 *mf*

14 *rit.*   *f*

6.14 HEY!

TRACK 3 48

ON THE PODIUM

Allegro

f

Hey!

MORE ABOUT SYNCOPATION

You already know the quarter-half-quarter syncopation. The most common syncopated rhythm is eighth-quarter-eighth. Here the syncopation occurs on the accented upbeat quarter note.

6.21 DIES IRAE

Pesante

att. Thomas of Celano

6.22 LEAGUE OF SUPERHEROES

Allegro

THEORY

CHROMATIC SCALE

A **half step** is the smallest interval between two pitches. Two consecutive half steps make a **whole step**. The **chromatic scale** has thirteen notes going up and down in consecutive half steps.

6.23 CHROMATIC SCALE

no key signature!

half step   whole step

HISTORY

MUSIC

Georges Bizet (1838 – 1875) was a child prodigy from Paris who composed his first symphony in 1855 when he was just 16! In his short 36-year life, he wrote many different types of music but is best known for his operas. His most famous opera is *Carmen*.

ART

The Impressionistic style was all the rage in the art world. Edgar Degas had painted *In Concert Cafe*, *The Song of the Dog*. American realist painter Thomas Eakins completed the *Gross Clinic*, a very real rendition of a surgeon overseeing an operation to remove part of a diseased thighbone.

WORLD

Events in 1875 included the first organized indoor ice hockey game in Montreal, the running of the first Kentucky Derby, and the patent of the electric dental drill.

6.24 HABAÑERA (FROM CARMEN) – Duet *Where is the ostinato?*

Georges Bizet

Moderato

OPUS 6 ENCORE!

INTERPRETATION STATION

TRACK 3 59

Listen to CD 3 Track 59. For each musical example, decide if the melody is based on a **Scale** or an **Arpeggio**.
Circle the letter that corresponds with your answer.

1. S A   2. S A   3. S A   4. S A

SIMON "SEZ"

TRACK 3 60

Listen to CD 3 Track 60. You will hear a well-known piece. Listen first, sing it, then find the pitches on your instrument.
You can then play along with the accompaniment track that follows. Can you match the notes and style of the initial recording?

COMPOSER'S CORNER

Performers sometimes compose music on the spot while they are playing! This is called **improvisation.** There is an ostinato below.
Have a partner play it (or use CD 3 Track 61 as a background track) while you improvise. Use the guide notes to help you out. Have fun!
Note: The CD recording repeats 4 times.

"WHATEVER!"

TRACK 3 61

PENCIL POWER

On the staff below, notate the enharmonic for each note. See if you can figure out the bonus notes!

CURTAIN UP!

6.25 O CANADA

Canadian National Anthem
Calixa Lavallée, Sir Adolphe-Basile Routhier, and Justice R.S. Weir

TRACK 3 62

BB208BSN

CURTAIN UP!

6.26 CHORALE IN B♭ MAJOR
(ALLE MENSCHEN MÜSSEN STERBEN)

J. S. Bach

TRACK **3** 63

Andante

6.27 RABBLE ROUSER

Robert Sheldon

TRACK **3** 64

Allegro

6.28 PROCESSION OF THE CHAMPIONS

Brian Balmages

TRACK 3 65

BB208BSN

6.29 ROYAL MARCH OF THE LION
Instrumental Solo

Camille Saint-Saëns
arr. Brian Balmages

TRACK 3 66

Piano Accompaniment

Note: Sections are repeated in the accompaniment for spacing reasons and do not always follow the solo part.

TRACK 3 67

(Piano accompaniment only)

BB208BSN

SCALES AND TECHNIQUE

CONCERT B♭ MAJOR

SCALE

SCALE IN THIRDS

CONCERT E♭ MAJOR

SCALE

SCALE IN THIRDS

CONCERT A♭ MAJOR

SCALE

SCALE IN THIRDS

CONCERT F MAJOR

SCALE

SCALE IN THIRDS

CHROMATIC SCALE

BB208BSN

RHYTHM REVIEW – OPUS 1-6

PRACTICING TIPS

Some exercises will be very easy for you to master while others will require more diligent practice. Be prepared to spend more time on the music that is difficult for you. Above all, be consistent in your approach and always end with something fun! The enclosed CDs are a great tool to help you practice, but it is important that you also practice alone.

- Find a **quiet place** where you can practice without distraction.

- Practice at the **same time each day** so it becomes part of your daily schedule.

- Use a **straight back chair** and a **music stand** to promote good posture.

- Begin with a **regular warm-up routine**.

- Practice your **lesson assignments** and **band music**, spending additional time on challenging sections.

- Wrap up your practice by playing **something fun**!

Photograph courtesy of Yamaha Corporation of America

○ = open

● = pressed down

◐ = half hole

INDEX